PERFORMANCE REVIEWS:
Why We Hate Them And What You Can Do About It!

By: Tim Moran

Former protector of the HR status quo

<u>*Dedication*</u>

For all of you who have received and/or delivered a crummy performance review. May this book give you hope for a better way.

Table of Contents

Chapter 6: Additional Process Questions   **57**

Chapter 7: Connecting The Merit Increase To The Performance Rating   **61**

INTRODUCTION

Perhaps no process sends a collective shudder through an organization — employees and managers alike — than the performance review process. When that email hits your inbox stating it's time to start performance reviews, the reaction is usually a series of moans, groans, and gasps combined with statements like "Oh, no," "Oh, crap," "Already?," "Kill me," or "Not now (please God, not ever)!"

When I was contemplating retiring from Hallmark and determining the timing of my actual retirement date, I honestly thought about performance review due dates and how I could get out of that painful process! How messed-up was that? It was a factor in my thinking about my retirement timing! If I could, I wanted to avoid that process if at all possible. (It didn't work out. I had to do my mid-year reviews for my folks. I'm glad I did them, and I'm glad I don't have to do them ever again!)

MAN ON A MISSION

I'm on a mission … a mission to significantly change the current conventional performance management/review process. My mission is to make it more concise, make it more effective, make it more efficient, make it more relevant.

For 30-plus years I've watched this jacked-up process spread through, smother and consume organizations like *The Blob*. It is the black hole of resource waste, the reason why we hate HR, the stank in stanky management.

I have a better way, not a perfect way, but a better way. Better than this mess we have today.

The Blob is a 1958 American horror/sci-fi film that depicts a giant amoeba-like alien that came from outer space and terrorizes a small community in Pennsylvania. The blob grows in size every time it consumes something in its path. (1) It gets bigger, scarier and more uncontrollable over time ... you know, just like the performance review process!

CHAPTER 1

Performance Management Beginnings And Current State

A. A Very Brief History Of Performance Management

Fredrick Winslow Taylor, the father of scientific management, is kind-of credited with the first performance-management process based on his time and motion studies in the early 1900s with steel workers. Scientific-management methods called for optimizing the way tasks were performed and simplifying the jobs enough so workers could be trained to perform their specialized sequence of motions in the one "best" way. (2) This allowed Taylor to measure performance and greatly improve the productivity of the steel workers.

While scientific-management principles improved productivity and had a substantial impact on industry, they also increased the monotony of work. The core job dimensions of skill variety, task identity, task significance, autonomy and feedback all were missing from the picture of scientific management. (3)

Doesn't make you feel that great about the origin of performance management.

In the 1950s Peter Drucker, management guru, taught Management By Objectives (MBO) and later described the technique in his 1954 book, *The Practice of Management*. It's interesting that Drucker developed this technique as a way to manage managers. It became popular in the 1960s and was abbreviated as MBO. It experienced both an upward and downward drift: it came to be applied to the organization as a whole and to employees below the managerial level. Today it has become so entrenched that in many corporations hundreds or thousands of employees labor — and still labor at least once yearly — in formulating MBO-type objectives. (4)

SMART goal setting evolved from Drucker's MBO concept. SMART goals are an acronym that stands for goals that are: **Specific**, **Measurable**, **Actionable**, **Relevant** and **Time-Bound**. I researched the origin of this concept and found no one in particular has been given credit for this method of goal setting. (5) In addition, SMART goals take a considerable amount of time to write, are very detailed and assume the business environment will stay fairly static during the year. This just isn't the case. Things change quickly and often. A critical flaw in SMART goal setting is not accounting for the dynamic nature of today's business world.

This is a brief history of performance management. Basically we are using performance management concepts that are 60 years old and have morphed into something bigger, more unwieldy and more complicated than their original intent.

B. Does Every Company Have A Performance Management Process?

Yes! Whether it is a formal, sophisticated process or an informal, unsophisticated process, every company has a performance management process. Some don't even know they have one.

Everyone evaluates performance ... somehow, someway. So even if you are in a small company and don't have a formal, written-down performance-management process, you have one. It might be highly subjective and not terribly effective, but you have one.

C. The "Normal" Performance Management Process Practiced Today

I'm going to be generalizing a bit because performance management comes in all shapes and sizes just like corporations come in all shapes and sizes. But the following is the "normal or standard" process followed by some small, and many medium and large companies today.

1. Goals/objectives are developed by the executive leadership team based on the business challenges and opportunities in the company's performance year.

2. These goals/objectives are cascaded down through the organization via various communication vehicles to create top-down alignment within the organization. Alignment = what I am working on should be in sync with what is important to the company.

3. The manager, with the knowledge of the top-down goals/objectives of the organization, works with her/his employees to develop specific objectives for each employee during the coming performance year.

4. The manager and employee take significant time to develop SMART (Specific, Measurable, Actionable, Relevant and Time-Bound) objectives. The objectives must be detailed. The employee must know exactly what she needs to do to hit the various performance ratings. The objective-setting process can go through several iterations.

5. The manager and employee "sign-off" on the performance goals/objectives.

6. Formal performance reviews are then conducted twice during the year. Once at mid-year to see if the employee is on track and the second is at the end of the year. The year-end review is the one that "counts."

7. For both the mid-year and year-end review, employees are asked to provide their input for the review. Most of the time this results in the following: the employee writes how they think they performed on each objective and assigns their ratings. The manager reads the employee's input, edits/revises it based on their perspective, and then assigns the final ratings for each objective and an overall rating.

8. A one-half hour to one-hour meeting takes place between the employee and manager. This is when the actual review is delivered to the employee. The manager and employee go over the review, discussing the employee's performance and the ratings.

9. Assuming no issues, the manager and employee sign the review. The reviews are sent to HR and become part of the personnel file.

10. Merit increases are given to employees based on the performance rating they receive.

11. Everybody goes home happy!

What a great process! Love and joy all-around the corporate world!

It makes sense, doesn't it? It's a logical, rationale process. So why does everyone hate it? Why do we resist and dread it?

It's simple; the world has changed *DRAMATICALLY* …

CHAPTER 2

So What's Changed In The World?

A. Change At Warp Speed

The speed of everything! (And the impact it has on everyone's time.)

The unbelievable change in technology capabilities over the last 30 years is mind-boggling, and it ain't slowing down. In fact, it is accelerating, as hard as that is to believe.

> *How fast is fast?*
>
> *Every day, we create 2.5 quintillion bytes of data — so much that 90% of the data in the world today has been created in the last two years alone. (6)*

I remember in 1982 when our manufacturing plant was introduced to word processing machines. That was a big deal! In 1984, or around then, desktop PCs started to appear. In 1995, the Internet started to really take off. In 2000, cell phones were becoming mainstream. And the list goes on … and on … and on …

All of these technology capabilities are allowing amazing gains in productivity, innovation and killer competition from every direction around the world. The business environment is global, dynamic, competitive and unpredictable; both externally and internally. Real-time communication, the ability to exchange data and have the tools to analyze data, transform data into useful information and make fast decisions … some tactical, but some highly strategic … that's our business reality. Literally the world is at our fingertips and if you are too slow, you will not survive.

Time-starved managers and employees are working under incredible pressure just to keep up with their work. The work environment is dynamic, unpredictable, uncertain and schizophrenic. What you thought were the most important things to accomplish in December or January (your SMART objectives) for the coming year could be irrelevant by February or March!

It's not your fault. It's not my fault. It's just the way it is. And there is no "pause" button.

*Talk about unpredictable and uncertain ... remember Bear Stearns? The company was founded in 1923. From **2005-2007**, Bear Stearns was recognized as the "Most Admired" securities firm in Fortune's "America's Most Admired Companies" survey, and second overall in the security firm section. The annual survey is a prestigious ranking of employee talent, quality of risk management and business innovation. This was the second time in three years that Bear Stearns had achieved this "top" distinction. By 2008 due to a series of poor executive decisions, Bear Stearns was sold to JP Morgan for a fraction of its previous value. **By 2010 JP Morgan ceased using the Bear Stearns name!** (7)*

B. What Else Has Changed?

Because of competitive pressures, expectations of companies have changed. Companies want more and more from their employees. Organizations are doing more with fewer resources ... constantly. You ever hear, "Work smarter not harder?" I bet you have. And as much as I want to punch the dudes in the head that said that to me, there is truth in this statement.

Companies need people who can think and do their jobs with minimal direction. They need people who can produce maximum value with minimal guidance. They need people who can self-manage their performance and understand everything cannot and will not be spelled out for them when it comes to articulating performance expectations.

When you are hired into an organization, it is ideal if you receive a job description. Even better if your manager sits down with you and discusses your role and expectations. Even "more better" if you receive training. But the reality is this may not happen. When you are hired to do a job it's up to you to figure out what that job is and how it can add value and make a difference within an organization. Do what the role requires and then do more. Developing, expanding and making your role more impactful are your job. Get used to it.

CHAPTER 3

The Milk's Gone Bad

A. Why The Old System Is Broken

The traditional performance management process has simply not kept up with the hyper dynamic business environment we face today and will face in the future. The old system was built on a management command-and-control model. Things were more stable and the business world was more predictable. More time could be and was spent on setting static objectives, diving into mindless and irrelevant details, communicating exactly what needed to be done by when … with lots of checks along the way. The dreaded mid-year and/or year-end performance reviews were the final result of this management process.

> *There's something profoundly wrong with a system when the only time you look at your objectives during the year is when you have a performance review.*

Time just doesn't allow this process to continue. The "standard" performance management process isn't effective. It's too slow, too complicated and too cumbersome. The performance review process has dragged organizations down and brought them to their knees when it kicked-in. It's hard to name another process that spawns such negative energy within an organization or sucks up so much time for so little payback. At Hallmark, I used the following graphic to illustrate what happens at performance review time:

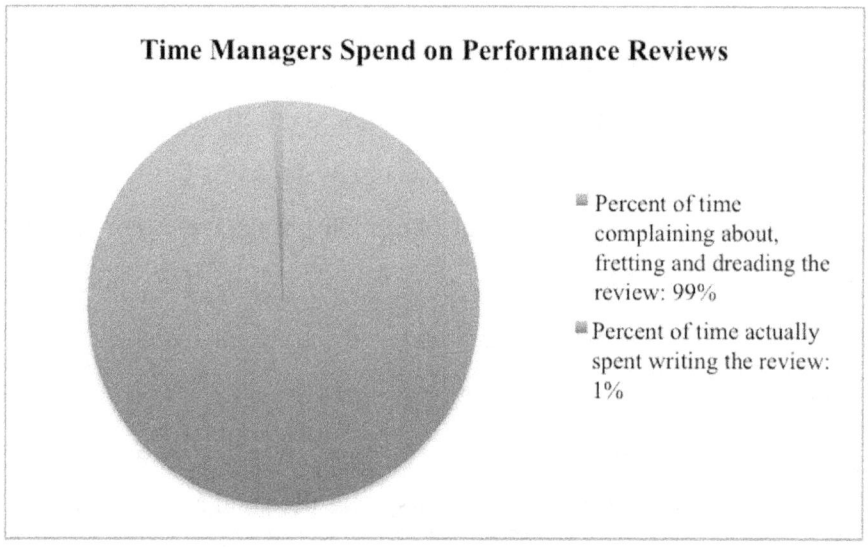

Time Managers Spend on Performance Reviews

- Percent of time complaining about, fretting and dreading the review: 99%
- Percent of time actually spent writing the review: 1%

In addition, several automated performance review solutions have emerged on the market. The issues with these solutions are:

- Automating a poor process isn't helpful.
- Most managers and employees use the automated system once or twice a year and they get frustrated with learning and re-learning how to use the system.
- The time savings these systems proclaim are questionable at best.

B. The "Normal" Performance Management Process Practiced Today And Why There Are Issues

In Chapter 1, C., I outlined the "normal or standard" performance management process followed by some small, and many medium and large companies today. Below in **bold** are the issues with the current process.

1. Goals/objectives are developed by the executive leadership team based on the business challenges and opportunities in the company's performance year. *Sometimes this is done well and many times it is not. Sometimes this is done in a timely manner and many times it is not. Sometimes it is clear what the leadership team is focusing on and often it is as clear as mud.*

2. These goals/objectives are cascaded down through the organization via various communication vehicles to create top-down alignment within the organization. Alignment = what I am working on should be in sync with what is important to the company. *Many times the communication is slow and due to corporate speak, not real clear. The average employee has a hard time understanding what the company is truly focusing on in the coming year and how it relates to their daily work.*

3. The manager, with the knowledge of the top-down goals/objectives of the organization, works with her/his

employees to develop specific objectives for each employee during the coming performance year. *Often, the manager's understanding of the top-down goals/objectives is not very clear and or isn't very relevant to her and her team. She isn't bashful about letting her employees know. I've heard several times during my career, "I don't know why we have to do this. I'm not sure how this pertains to our jobs. Somehow we have to try and tie these together. I hate HR."*

4. The manager and employee take significant time to develop SMART (Specific, Measurable, Actionable, Relevant and Time-Bound) objectives. The objectives must be detailed. The employee must know exactly what she/he needs to do to hit the various performance ratings. The objective setting process can go through several iterations. *Mercy me, where do I begin? Many managers do not work with their employees to write objectives. They delegate this to the employee and edit what the employee gives them. Some managers barely read them or don't read them at all. And good luck trying to articulate exactly what a person needs to do to receive a specific rating. It's probably possible to do this when things are quantifiable. But many things just don't lend themselves to being quantified. Some employees want to know exactly how I will get measured and rated. I've got news for them, it isn't feasible, it isn't practical and*

it will always be an inexact measure. That is a business reality and as much as we don't like it … it is what it is.

5. The manager and employee "sign-off" on the performance goals/objectives. *Many times this is done just to get it done versus a true meeting of the minds. There isn't a joint understanding of the objectives to be accomplished in the coming year.*

6. Formal performance reviews are then conducted twice during the year. Once at mid-year to see if the employee is on track and the second is at the end of the year. The year-end review is the one that "counts." *The once- or twice-a-year scramble that occurs organization-wide is a sorry sight to behold.*

7. For both the mid-year and year-end review, employees are asked to provide their input for the review. Most of the time this results in the following: the employee writes how they think they performed on each objective and assigns their ratings. The manager reads the employee's input, edits/revises it based on their perspective, and then assigns the final ratings for each objective and an overall rating. *Is it just me or does it seem odd that the employee writes her own review and the manager edits it and slaps a rating on it? I dun'no … just seems kind of weird, but it is widely accepted. Things that can and do happen: sometimes the manager barely reads and/or edits the employee's input. I know this from first-hand*

experience. If you and your boss do not talk throughout the year, the manager's rating can come out of left field. The one good thing about ratings, they do let you know what your manager thinks about your performance— right, wrong or indifferent.

8. A one half-hour to one-hour meeting takes place between the employee and manager. This is when the actual review is delivered to the employee. The manager and employee go over the review, discussing the employee's performance and the ratings. *For a lot of people, this is the longest half hour or hour of their year. Some managers read the review and the ratings to their employee word for word, kind of like Chinese water torture. Some managers just ask the employee if they have any questions, wanting to get through the meeting as quickly as possible without a battle. "Having a meaningful dialogue" is not how I would describe most of these meetings. It is rarely a discussion.*

9. Assuming no issues, the manager and employee sign the review. The reviews are sent to HR and become part of the personnel file. *Most of the time there aren't issues because both parties just want to be done with it. However, there are those managers who do a really poor job of this and employees do take them to task. And there are some employees who have very poor self-awareness and have a highly inflated view of*

themselves. This is where the real fun begins. The employee relations police have a case and are called in to investigate!

10. Merit increases are given to employees based on the performance rating they receive. *Oh man, if this was only true! HR produces merit-increase guide charts based on the employee's performance rating and where the employee is relative to the compensation range of their job. Based on where the employee is on this grid determines her/his percentage salary increase. Managers use judgment and discretion in this process. And, they normally just screw this up! I can't tell you how exposed companies are based on the willy-nilly nature of how managers use or don't use these guide charts. It is so sad and maddening.*

11. Everybody goes home happy! *No freaking way.*

C. Why We Hate It

I think you're getting the picture of why so many people hate the performance review process. That goes for those writing and delivering the reviews and for those receiving them.

But let me just hit some of the highlights:

1. Generally speaking, most people do not like to be judged, evaluated and critiqued. The older you get, I think the truer this becomes.

2. Fear of the unknown. My manager and I haven't really talked about my performance per se throughout the year. I have no idea what he/she really thinks of me.

3. The performance review has retarded daily conversations regarding performance. "I'll wait to discuss this with her at performance review time," is something I overheard consistently. Translation, "I will break out the hammer on her during the performance review."

4. The entire review process takes a lot of time or is perceived to take a lot of time.

5. Although "feedback is a gift," most of us prefer feedback that is positive versus constructive, negative or developmental. Just tell me I'm great! I'd really prefer not to hear about my development areas or weaknesses. I can't tell you how many times I had people say to me, "Give it to me straight" and, I did, and, they got ticked off. I have found that most people can't handle the truth.

6. Most people have: average – to below average – to poor – self-awareness.

7. Trust in your manager is a major concern for many employees. Do I trust the person making judgments about

26

me? Does she care about me and have my best interests in mind?

8. Top-down and cascading objectives — although good in theory — lose their relevancy as they filter down into the organization.

9. In some organizations, the start of the "normal" process is to have you write your own objectives. You're lucky if your boss is mildly involved or engaged in setting your objectives. It's rare to have a boss who reads, critiques and edits your objectives, and has "an actual meeting of the minds" to really decide on objectives.

10. SMART objectives are too detailed and cumbersome. If you both have to be that specific, I need a new leader and a new employee.

11. Sometimes your objectives make no sense and have nothing to do with your role. Ever have a diversity objective? I've heard of customer service reps who have leadership objectives ... you're killin' me Smalls.

12. Two or three months into the year, everything has changed and your priorities have completely changed. However, your objectives are set in stone like the Ten Commandments. They aren't relevant. But, come review time, by gosh, you better had done everything or else.

13. Most managers are flat-out lame at doing any part of this process, and they don't want to do it.

14. You are asked to provide input on your review. Translation: Write your own review, your manager edits it (sometimes missing key points) and slaps a rating on it. Wow, thanks for the effort boss!

15. Sometimes the boss rarely sees you in action. She relies on others or your self-report to evaluate you. Really? Yes, really.

16. The actual performance review meeting becomes a battle of wills. The manager armed with her ammunition and the employee scared, uncertain but ready to fight for that 1.25% merit increase!

17. Sometimes HR or management determines a finite percentage of performance ratings the organization will allow. It's called forced ranking. For example, in a department of 10, only so many people can receive a high rating, only so many can receive a middle rating, and so many must receive a low rating. Managers are forced to make stuff up or over emphasize a shortcoming so they can downgrade an employee's performance. Talk about demoralizing, demotivating and cut-throat. One of the worst ideas ever invented.

D. Why Do We Defend It So?

We've all been duped and brain-washed. This is how we do it in American business. It's a jacked-up process. We all hate it, but let's keep doing it because …

- 'Cause it is what we know. It's what we have grown up with.
- 'Cause as much as it sucks, we are comfortable with it.
- It makes us (HR) feel good, like we are making a difference. Like we are aligned with the company goals and objectives. It gives us purpose, it gives us power, it lets us analyze data, it takes time, it makes us feel important. Please! What a bunch of bull!
- 'Cause coming up with a better way is perceived to be hard.
- 'Cause thinking of a better way requires courage and vision.

You can count on HR, HR consultants, and lame line leaders to defend this process to the bitter end. It's like a snake you run over several times and when you get out of your car to check it, that thing is still alive!

CHAPTER 4

Ideas For A Better Way

A. Executive Leadership

If your CEO and executive leadership team are not on-board to have a formal performance management process, DO NOT DO IT!

What does this mean? They must be visibly supportive and do it! They must understand, communicate and follow the process. It's even better if they are champions of the process, e.g., taking the time to discuss the importance of great performance to the organization and how this process will help drive a winning company. They must lead by example. If the process is good enough for them to communicate and support, then they must follow it, too. No exceptions.

Word travels fast when the executive leadership team doesn't practice what they preach. Their credibility and the process go out the window.

> *There are much easier and far less time-consuming ways to tick your employees off then dragging them through an over-complicated performance review process.*

Let me provide you with a few real life personal examples illustrating why employees become cynical and distrusting of this process.

Exhibit A

Ned (not his real name) was the head of an HR department. One of his responsibilities was developing the performance management process for the entire organization. He was responsible for developing and preaching the importance of performance management and ensuring the organization embraced the process. I reported directly to Ned. He was a great guy, but he didn't do his performance reviews for his people. Or, when he did do them, he would be three-six months late. This was the same guy I would see spewing at the mouth about the importance of managing performance and hammering on those managers who didn't do it.

Exhibit B

At a former company of mine, we had an automated performance review process. This automated system allowed you to go on-line and write your performance reviews at mid-year (and year-end). This particular situation occurred during the mid-year process. The timeline for completing the mid-year performance reviews was the following:

June – Employees provide input for their review.

July – The manager writes the reviews.

August – The manager delivers the reviews.

By August 31 – Reviews must be electronically submitted with performance ratings. The system is shut down and you can't submit reviews after August 31.

Pretty straightforward. I was aware of a situation where an executive wrote the reviews just in the nick of time and submitted them through the automated system. He didn't bother to go over them with his employees until September. I think some might have dragged into October.

So, let me recap. He wrote the reviews and sent them in so he wouldn't be dinged for not getting them in on time. He did this without talking to any of his direct reports about the content of the reviews or the performance ratings.

This was the same executive who spoke in front of large employee groups telling everyone about the virtues and importance of managing performance, writing reviews and explaining how it was important to sit with your employees and have a dialogue with each of them about their performance.

Exhibit C

A former boss of mine asked us to write our objectives for the coming year. He was interested in knowing what we wanted to accomplish before telling us what he wanted us to accomplish. I was cool with that.

I was young at the time and relatively new in my career. I was kind of a smart ass, too, so as a joke, I wrote an objective that said, "Mastery of the Crane Technique," … you know, from *The Karate Kid.* I'm dating myself, but that movie was popular at the time. I went on to describe how I would work on my balance, kicking technique, etc.

About a week or so after I submitted my objectives, much to my surprise, my boss told me he had read my objectives and agreed with all of them. I really didn't know what to say. If I told him I had written a bogus objective as a joke, I would be calling him out 'cause he didn't read them. I had only been with the company a relative short period of time (approximately six months).

Anyway, I ended up changing the document, re-printing it and giving it to him for my permanent file. I made up an excuse that

I had found a typo and wanted to ensure we had a grammatically correct document on file. Holy crapola!

Exhibit D

At one of my former companies, the leadership team and HR became frustrated with managers not completing reviews on time. So, here's the idea we came up with. If a manager did not complete her review on time, the employee's merit increase would be withheld until the review was completed and given. Yes, you heard this right! The employee was penalized monetarily for the manager not doing her job! You can't make this stuff up. Being a part of the HR team (I was at a very low-level at the time) I argued vehemently about how crazy this idea was and how we were penalizing the wrong person(s). You'd think I was talking to a tree.

Well, we did implement this crazy policy. I think it lasted about a month or two until employees threatened a mutiny or to put the kybosh on their lame managers who were tardy with their reviews.

If your CEO and executives are on-board to have a formal process and they are going to actively participate and support the process, then proceed.

B. The Importance Of Clear And Authentic Communication

Once the executive team is on-board, I would suggest an open-and-honest communication to the organization that would look something like this:

1. We are going to have a formal performance management process.
2. Everyone in the organization will participate in this process, especially the leadership of the company.
3. It will be simple, direct and fast.
4. We must be able to move fast because of the dynamic nature of our business today.
5. We will not spend a lot of time writing detailed objectives. We trust you and your manager to know your jobs and to know the most important things to work on.
6. We will encourage and expect our mangers to coach performance daily. "Coaching in the moment" is our new way of doing things.
7. Your self-awareness and willingness to receive and accept feedback are critical to make this process work.
8. The formal performance review will be a practical recap of performance with ratings. Performance ratings will be given by the manager based on her perception of your performance.
9. There will be no forced ranking of performance. Said another way, you will get the rating you earn.

10. If we are able to allocate merit increases based on company performance, they will be consistent across departments for the rating achieved.
11. We need everyone on-board with this process. Being a performance-driven organization is critical to our success.

C. Organization Discipline

I can't stress enough the importance of organization discipline in making this process work. Everyone must lock arms and be committed to doing the reviews on time and to the best of their ability. Once you allow a manager to miss the deadline for a review to be completed and delivered, you undermine the entire system. It's real simple to make it work ... implement clear consequences for not completing and delivering reviews on time and stick to them. The leadership team will either make this happen or not. There is no gray here.

D. Defining Performance (What + How)

Before moving forward with a better way to manage performance, there needs to be agreement on the definition of performance. There is a lot of clutter around how to define it. In reality, it's pretty easy to define.

Performance is the following:

What you do (**Results**) + how you do it (**Behaviors**) = Performance

That's it. It's no more complicated than that. But man, every corporate knucklehead with skin in the game will try and often succeed in making it way more complicated than this.

What you accomplish will always be more important than how you accomplished it.* That is to say, we may not like someone's personality, but in the end, it is the results that matter.

> *The one caveat: There must be an acceptable level of honesty, integrity and ethics. (Examples: Lance Armstrong had his seven Tour De France titles stripped from him (results) because he was found guilty of doping (how). Pete Rose is the all-time Major League hit leader (results), but is permanently banned from baseball due to gambling allegations (how).*

E. How Do You Measure And Evaluate The "What"?

So how do you measure and evaluate the "what" of performance? There are three components to measure the "what:"

Quality – You need to measure and evaluate the quality of the work.

Quantity (productivity) – You need to measure and evaluate how much is produced.

Timeliness – You need to measure and evaluate the timeliness of the work.

Ideas for Assessing the Quality of the Work:

1. What was accomplished? What results were achieved versus what was expected from the role?

2. How significant was their contribution? What was the impact? Was the impact at the job, department, division, company or enterprise level?

3. What impact did their work have on driving revenue or decreasing costs? (The higher the individual's job level, the greater the impact should be.)

4. What was the level of their creative, innovative or critical thinking in producing the quality of their results?

5. Did they resolve a gnarly problem or situation that was complex? Did it result in solving a systemic, long-term problem or was it just a quick fix? Said another way, was it a strategic solution or a tactical fix?

6. Did they meet or exceed the quality standards established for the task?

7. Were there mistakes or errors made in accomplishing the tasks/results? Was rework required?

8. Did they take the initiative to resolve issues/situations/problems before they became bigger?

9. Did they anticipate problems and resolve them?

10. Did they ask good clarifying questions to enhance the quality of the work they did or did they just do what they were told?

Ideas for Assessing the Quantity of the Work:

1. How much work did they accomplish or produce versus what was expected?

2. Were they a top producer versus other employees in the department?

3. Did they take on more work than others?

4. Did they produce one-and-a-half times ... two times... or three times the work of a "normal" employee's output in the department?

5. Did they work efficiently and facilitate efficient work for others?

Ideas for Assessing the Timeliness of the Work:

1. Did they meet or beat deadlines on a consistent and regular basis?

2. Did they respond to requests with a high sense of urgency or did you feel they were someone you had to wait on or chase down?

3. Did they follow-up or follow-through with a high sense of urgency?

4. Did their timeliness influence, in a positive way, the timeliness of others getting work done?

F. How Do You Measure And Evaluate The "How"?

Probably no area has more judgment and controversy than trying to measure the "how" of performance. Measuring behaviors, competencies, soft skills, etc., can be very difficult and at times very inexact. However, it is a very important part of performance and not doing it because it is hard or imperfect is not a solution.

There are so many behaviors that can make up the "how" of performance. Instead of just listing all of them I've grouped them into similar behaviors. I'm hopeful this will be helpful to you.

The six groupings of behaviors are:

General work behavior

Handling conflict/feedback

Communication

Efficiency

Leadership

Ethic/integrity

General work behavior:

1. Were they good to work with? Thinking about how they acted and behaved, would you want to work with them again?

2. Were they a team player in good and bad situations?

3. Did they get done what they said they were going to get done, when they said they were going to get it done?

4. Were they a partner with a POV — did they have opinions and bring them forward? Did they actively participate?

5. Did they bring good critical thinking versus surface thinking to problems/situations?

6. Did they take initiative?

7. Did they go the extra mile to perform?

8. Were they reliable — could you count on them?

9. Did they keep confidences?

10. Could they laugh at themselves and help create a good work environment?

11. Did they bring and/or create positive energy or did they suck the life out of others?

12. Did they promote an environment where everyone wanted to contribute and be there?

Handling conflict/feedback:

1. Did they challenge or push back when they disagreed with a course of action? Did they do so professionally or act like a baby or jerk? Said another way, did they effectively handle and address conflict?
2. Could they take, deliver and receive feedback that was constructive?
3. Did they play the victim card?
4. Could they change their mind and compromise when it made sense — or, once set on a course of action were they stubborn and uncompromising?

Communication:

1. Did they communicate effectively? Did people understand them and were they able to make their point(s)?
2. Did they communicate efficiently and concisely or did they talk too much with nothing of substance to say?
3. Was their communication authentic, transparent and sincere?
4. Did they listen?

Efficiency:

1. Did they waste time or were they efficient?
2. Did they follow-up and follow-through?
3. Did they do their homework? Were they prepared?
4. Were they decisive?

Leadership:

1. Did they lead when leading was necessary?
2. Did they have a vision for what could be and did they sell it?
3. Did they see the bigger picture or did they get bogged down in details? Too much analysis paralysis?
4. Did they try to bring people along?
5. Did they influence?
6. Did they take action or just sit-back and let things happen?

Ethics/Integrity:

1. Did they perform their duties with honesty, integrity, and ethics?
2. Did they have the company's best interest in mind or their own?
3. Could you trust them? Did they do what they said they were going to do?

A Final Word About the "How" of Performance

I do not recommend evaluating *each* of these grouping when determining the "How" rating. I think this level of complexity is unnecessary. There are so many things that make up the "How" of performance as evidenced in the previous groupings. The degree of importance and relevancy of the "How" for each employee and position is highly dynamic.

For example, if someone is great to work with but is caught stealing, they won't be working for a company for very long. Even though many of their behaviors may have been effective, this one serious behavioral issue trumps all of the others. It's too hard to account for these various situations when evaluating the "How". I therefore offer the groupings of behaviors as a way to think about and evaluate the "How." And, to help you focus and pinpoint your performance discussion with an employee when discussing their behaviors. You and your employee should decide on the most relevant behaviors for their position. You should discuss them throughout the year, coach and provide feedback on them daily and formally evaluate them at mid-year and year-end with the one "How" rating.

CHAPTER 5

Putting It All Together

A. A Simple Performance Review Form

Let's start with a review of a simple performance review form. It is the foundation of the process and sets the tone for a concise, practical and fast performance management process. The simple performance review form:

PERFORMANCE REVIEW FORM

Employee's Name:	Employee's Job Title:
Reviewer's Name:	Reviewer's Job Title:
Review Period: From: To:	Date the Review was Delivered:

*Performance is evaluated based on **What** was accomplished (the results) and **How** it was accomplished (the behaviors demonstrated accomplishing the results).*

Performance of the employee's day-to-day responsibilities and significant projects, initiatives, goals, and/or objectives (if applicable) will be evaluated during the review period. Listed in the space provided below are significant projects, initiatives, goals, and/or objectives the employee has committed to complete during the performance year.

Please circle the rating number below that best describes the employee's performance on the four components. In addition, assign an overall performance rating.

The rating scale:
5 = Excellent
4 = Very Good
3 = Good
2 = Needs Improvement
1 = Unacceptable

Quality of work accomplished:
5 – 4 – 3 – 2 – 1
Quantity of work accomplished:
5 – 4 – 3 – 2 – 1
Timeliness of work accomplished:
5 – 4 – 3 – 2 – 1
Behaviors demonstrated accomplishing the work:
5 – 4 – 3 – 2 - 1

Overall performance review rating:

Performance review summary comments:

_____
_____
_____

Employee's Signature:	Date:
Reviewer's Signature:	Date:

B. Relevant Information

The first section of the review form contains the relevant information for the performance review: whom the review is for; who is giving it; and when did they give it. Of course, this can be tailored to fit your company's needs. I've provided you with what must be in this section.

C. Day-To-Day Responsibilities And Goals/Objectives

Previously we discussed performance has two components: What you do (Results) + how you do it (Behaviors) = Performance

We want to evaluate the employee in two areas:

(1) How they perform the day-to-day responsibilities of their job

All employees, at a minimum, are expected to do a "good" job performing the day-to-day responsibilities of their current position and being accountable for the results. This is very important to running an effective and efficient organization in the near-term.

Some things to consider regarding day-to-day responsibilities:

- Are there job descriptions?
- Are employees clear (as clear as they can be) regarding what they are responsible and accountable for? This will

never be 100%, but employees and managers should have a joint understanding of the daily responsibilities and accountabilities.

(2) How they perform on projects/initiatives/goals/objectives they and their manager have agreed upon.

In addition, in order to run a growing and sustainable enterprise in the long-term, most employees need to think beyond their day-to-day responsibilities. They need to think of new ways to improve how things are done in their job, department, division or the company. Therefore, at the start of the year, most employees and managers are expected to identify, commit to and complete projects and/or initiatives that will help drive positive change and improvement within their job, department, division or the company.

Regarding significant projects/initiatives/goals/objectives:

- Who should have these? Employees in positions where it makes sense! Some positions are lower level and just don't lend themselves to objective setting. And you know what, that's all right. For most positions though, you do want your employees to be thinking of things that will have a positive impact on the company beyond just doing their job.
- How many should they have? This depends on several factors. The level of the position, the complexity of the project/initiative, etc., are all factors.

- How detailed should they be? They should state the project/initiative/goal/objective to be completed and the date to be completed. Avoid SMART objectives and/or cumbersome detailed objectives. The objectives must be meaningful to the employee and manager. The acid test for the objective: both the employee and manager discuss it often because it is very important to accomplish. If neither remembers the objectives or discusses them until review time, they weren't very important things to accomplish.

- Can these be adjusted? Yes! Any time during the year. This is very important. As I have discussed throughout this book, the business environment is highly dynamic and things change. Adjusting objectives should be a natural and fluid part of the process.

D. The Scales And Descriptors

I've seen several scales during my years of experience. Pass/fail scales, three-point scales, and five-point scales. I even heard of a 26-point scale! (I never actually saw it, but I heard it existed in a company). I prefer and recommend a five-point scale. Why? I think it allows for the right amount of differentiation, and it's what we have grown up with and are used to from school ... the five-point grading scale of A, B, C, D or F. If you are trying to create a somewhat intuitive and easy-to-comprehend scale, then I highly recommend the five-point scale.

There are a lot of examples of scales and descriptors. I think using words that are intuitive and that people can easily comprehend leads to less confusion and better understanding when discussing performance with employees.

I recommend the following descriptors:

Excellent (5) – The work is excellent, the employee consistently performs well beyond what you would normally expect. Adjectives that best describe this work are: outstanding, superior, exceptional, great.

Very Good (4) – The work is very good, the employee consistently performs above what you would normally expect.

Good (3) – The work is good, the employee consistently performs and meets expectations. Adjectives that best describe this work: competent, skillful, solid.

Needs Improvement (2) – The work does not meet expectations, the employee consistently performs below expectations.

Unacceptable (1) – The work is poor and badly misses expectations.

E. Weighting

Like a lot of things regarding performance management and reviews, weighting objectives or sections in order to place emphasis on certain results, seems like a good idea. However, the execution of this idea, that is actually deciding what should be weighted and why and then doing the math, usually leads to errors, confusion and a general feeling of why the heck did we do this?

So in our model, I would not weight the four components of performance. Simply circle the number that best reflects the rating for that particular section.

Quality
Quantity
Timeliness
Behaviors (How)

The final Overall Rating would be determined by adding the scores from the four sections and then dividing them by four. I can't make the math any simpler.

F. Overall Performance Review Rating Scales

If you can add four numbers and divide them by four, then you can calculate and assign an overall performance rating. The following are the numerical ranges and the corresponding ratings.

Excellent =	4.5 - 5.0
Very good =	3.5 - 4.4
Good =	2.5 – 3.4
Needs Improvement =	1.5 – 2.4
Unacceptable =	< 1.4

G. Would You Allow Judgment When Assigning The Overall Performance Rating?

Yes, but only in rare situations, maybe less than 1% of the time. What are those situations you ask? When the employee is on the border of a rating and there is a compelling reason based on extraordinary effort, acts of God, etc. Be careful though, this can be a slippery slope. In almost 100% of the time, the math is the math and the rating is the rating.

I would require levels of review and approval all the way up to the executive leadership of the organization in order to make an exception.

H. The Summary Comments Section

The summary comments section is just that, a place for the manager (reviewer) to add her/his summary comments regarding the employee's performance during the review period. The comments should support the overall rating.

Some things to consider in this section:

- The words should reflect rating(s). For example, don't use "great job" if the employee received a "good" overall rating.
- Keep it short and simple. Less is more. The value of the review is in the conversation.
- Nothing, and I mean nothing, in the comment section, should refer to, directly or indirectly: race, color, religion, sex, national origin, age or disability.

Summary comments section examples:
- Josh had an excellent year! He far exceeded expectations and was great to work with. I appreciated his drive throughout the year and his willingness to tackle difficult problems. He helped bring about significant changes that positively impacted the company's performance. Thanks Josh, appreciate all you did!
- Erika performed well this year and overall earned a "good" performance rating. She met expectations and was a solid

team member. She continues to be a valued member of the department.

- Tate earned a "needs improvement" rating this year. As noted on the review, Tate's quality of work and timeliness of completing his work needs to improve in order for him to continue in his role. We will be working on a development plan to address these concerns.

I. Signing And Dating The Review

At the end of the review, there is a place for the employee and manager to sign and date the review. This is acknowledging the performance appraisal was presented and reviewed on the date of the signatures. The employee's signature on the review does not mean the employee agrees with the review/ratings. Over the years I ran into several situations where the employee did not agree with the review and their rating and refused to sign it. That's okay. In those situations, the manager just needs to write on the review that the employee refused to sign it. (*Note: This is typically a red flag for the manager and/or HR. It is well worth the time to find out the reason(s) why the employee refused to sign the review. There are likely to be deeper issues between the employee and manager that need to be addressed.*)

J. Several Examples Of Performance Ratings And The Math

Sorry everyone, you will have to do some math or automate the math on your performance review form.

Excellent Performer Example:

Quality = **5** (= an "excellent" rating)

Quantity = **4** (= a "very good" rating)

Timeliness = **4** (= a "very good" rating)

Behaviors (How) = **5** (= an "excellent" rating)

Total Performance Evaluation Points = 18

Total Perf. Eval. Avg. Score = 4.5 (18/4 = 4.5)
4.5 = Excellent Performance

Very Good Performer Example:

Quality = **5** (= an "excellent" rating)

Quantity = **4** (= a "very good" rating)

Timeliness = **4** (= a "very good" rating)

Behaviors (How) = **4** (= a "very good" rating)

Total Performance Evaluation Points = 17

Total Perf. Eval. Avg. Score = 4.25 (17/4 = 4.25)
4.25 = Very Good Performance

Good Performer Example:

Quality = **3** (= a "good" rating)

Quantity = **3** (= a "good" rating)

Timeliness = **4** (= a "very good" rating)

Behaviors (How) = **3** (= a "good" rating)

Total Performance Evaluation Points = 13

Total Perf. Eval. Avg. Score = 3.25 (13/4 = 3.25)
3.25 = Good Performance

Needs Improvement Performer Example:

Quality = **2** (= "needs improvement" rating)

Quantity = **2** (= a "needs improvement" rating)

Timeliness = **2** (= a "needs improvement" rating)

Behaviors = **3** (= a "good" rating)

Total Performance Evaluation Points = 9

Total Perf. Eval. Avg. Score = 2.25 (9/4 = 2.25)
2.25 = Needs Improvement Performance

Unacceptable Performer Example:

Quality = **1** (= an "unacceptable" rating)

Quantity = **1** (= an "unacceptable" rating)

Timeliness = **2** (= a "needs improvement" rating)

Behaviors (How) = **1** (= an "unacceptable" rating)

Total Performance Evaluation Points = 5

Total Perf. Eval. Avg. Score = 1.25 (5/4 = 1.25)
1.25 = Unacceptable Performance

CHAPTER 6

Additional Process Questions

A. How Often Should You Conduct Formal Performance Reviews?

With this process and format, I would recommend conducting reviews a minimum of twice per year. Formal reviews are like truth serum between the employee and manager. Regardless of the many conversations (hopefully many) the employee and manager have during a performance year, an accounting of this process with a formal rating clears up any ambiguity that either might have regarding performance.

If there are differences of opinions, concerns, ideas for improvement, ideas for better communication, etc., I would much rather know about them and address them at mid-year versus the end of the year when there is no time to course correct actions by either party.

In an ideal world/environment with this process, I would recommend once per quarter, especially if this process can be automated.

B. Would You Have Employees Rate Themselves?

I would strongly recommend employees rating themselves. There is great value in having employees provide their input in terms of a self-rating. This provides employees with an opportunity to:

- Give their input and let their manager know how they view themselves.
- Demonstrate their ability to critically and objectively evaluate themselves, thus demonstrating their level of self-awareness.
- Demonstrate potential management and leadership skills through their self-evaluation skill.
- Have a "meeting of the minds" with their manager regarding the definition of the ratings and what they actually mean.

Employees need to understand however, they are providing their input and the manager is the final evaluator and decision maker. Said another way, this is not a democratic process. The employee's input is just that, input.

Early in my career, one of my first managers gave me the opportunity to rate myself. We then compared my self-ratings versus the ratings he had given me. It was eye-opening and a hard meeting for me. I was early in my career, just a few years out of college, and thought I was pretty much great at everything. We were disconnected; me rating myself higher (and in some cases) much higher than he had rated me. It was humbling. I was ticked off and listened as best I could to his rationale.

As painful as this experience was for me, it did several things:

- It gave us a common ground for understanding what the ratings meant.
- It gave me an understanding of where I was and what I needed to do or change to get better.
- It gave me a better understanding of myself.
- It made me reflect on my performance and my career, where I was and where I wanted to be.
- It helped me "grow up" in the business world.

C. Would You Have Others Rate Them?

Because this system is not onerous, I would also recommend asking other people who work closely with the employee to provide their feedback on her/him using the simple performance review form and providing their comments to the manager. I like the idea of asking the employee for the people they would recommend the manager ask for employee input. However, and this is a strong however, the manager has the final say regarding the employees she will solicit for input. Why? Because in some cases, the employee does not provide an objective list of evaluators. That's okay as long as the employee understands he/she is making a recommendation regarding who to ask for input and the manager makes the final decision on who will be asked.

Other things to consider:

- If employees provide their input, I would let them know their feedback will be anonymous. Why? I think you will get more realistic feedback from them.
- I would recommend asking 3-5 people for their feedback. This should be enough to provide a balanced picture of the perceived performance of the individual.
- Remember this is feedback regarding the person based on perception. Hopefully, the feedback will validate the manager's view of the person's performance. If there are big discrepancies between the manager's perception and those providing input, it is an opportunity for the manager to re-examine their ratings and evaluation.
- Feedback from others is just that, feedback. The ultimate decision on the performance ratings is the manager's.

CHAPTER 7

Connecting The Merit Increase To The Performance Rating

A. Would You Tie The Performance Rating To The Merit Increase?

Abso-freaking-lutely! If you are not going to tie pay to performance, then your best move would be to a socialist society versus one based on capitalism and competition. An organization and the livelihood of all those in the organization depends on the performance of the organization. The performance of the organization is based on the individual performance of everyone in the organization. Those who produce the best results receive the highest percentage pay increases. Period. End-of-story.

B. How Would You Tie Merit Increases To The Performance Review Ratings?

I would make it formulaic. Sadly, over time, managers have proven time and time again they cannot effectively manage a merit budget. Their ability to differentiate, that is, giving the biggest percentage of the pie to their top performers, has been average to below average at best. Because the merit pools are so small, I think many managers revert to trying to give everyone something, to the detriment of their best performers. On one level, I certainly get this; on another level, it undermines rewarding your top performers.

In addition, from a legal standpoint, when managers exercise poor judgment with regard to how they determine pay increases, it puts the company at risk. If an employee in a protected class would challenge the company (manager) and file a charge of discrimination based on the percentage increase given or not given, good luck defending it, 'cause you are going to need it.

Benefits of using a merit increase formula:

- Makes the process more consistent and objective for managers and employees. Each knows what to expect. It is fairer and less subjective. A performance rating = an increase amount ... period.

- Saves a tremendous amount of management and HR time. HR can quit making those freaking guide charts and managers can quit trying to figure them out (and in some cases manipulate them.)

- For managers who want to reward their buddies, this helps put a governor on them.

- You can still allow flexibility and reward top performers with spot bonuses if they are above the salary range for a job grade.

An Example of How a Standard Merit Increase Process Would Work:

The size of the merit pool will help you determine your merit formula. An example of a merit pool formula for a 2% merit pool could look something like this:

Excellent =	3% merit increase
Very Good =	2% merit increase
Good =	1% merit increase
Needs Improvement =	No merit increase
Unacceptable =	No merit increase

I presented this idea when I was at Hallmark. My compensation partners were not in favor of this process at all. Their argument: how can you publish a formula upfront when you don't know the ratings? My argument back to them was:

- Look at last year's ratings distribution in the company.
- Look at the company's historical ratings distribution (say the last three years).
- Analyze how the company is performing in the current year (using some judgment).
- Develop a projected ratings-distribution model based on the three variables above.

- From the projected ratings-distribution model, determine what the projected merit increases will be for the ratings in the performance year.

- Communicate this upfront to the entire organization with the following caveat: If the projected ratings distribution model is materially different than the actual ratings distribution, then a new merit formula will be developed and communicated to the entire organization. In this way, the company is protected for over or under paying for performance based on the uncertainty of how the actual distribution turns out.

Final Thoughts

The performance review process might be the most despised process in American business today. I've provided the reasons for that and what you can do to make it better. To borrow a line from the AT&T commercial, "It's not complicated." It will take some guts to divert from the crowd and use a far less complicated, but still highly effective and efficient process.

Many of my colleagues and friends in HR will write this off as too simple, not sophisticated enough and not strategic. That's fine. At the end of the day, all an organization needs is an effective and practical tool to evaluate an employee's performance. The organization also needs the courage, self-discipline and resolve to follow their process. In a world where speed is of the essence and ambiguity rules, a straightforward process without the barnacles of HR jibber-jabber can be very effective.

In the end, the formal performance review process will never take the place of authentic conversations about performance. The performance review is a "report card" of how the employee performed during a certain period of time in an organization. Coaching in the moment ... recognizing and praising good performance, pinpointing and coaching employees when they are missing the mark, doing this with honesty, sincerity and truthfulness ... this is the glue that binds outstanding organizations.

<u>Acknowledgements</u>

I've wanted to write this book for a long-time. I'm so grateful to have had the time to finally get it done.

I want to thank my wife Pat, my son Josh and my daughter Erika for your encouragement, reading the first draft of this book and providing your honest feedback. There's nothing like trying out your writing on your family. Love you.

Thank you to Diane McCaffrey for her editing skills. And thank you to cover designer Craig Lueck. Appreciate the work you both did.

To my two dogs, Max and Tate, thanks for hanging out with me on a daily basis as I was grinding through the writing and editing. Max, appreciate your quiet sleeping. Tate, your snoring was intolerable at times but you were still cool to hang out with.

And finally, I'd like to thank all of my past companies, managers and fellow employees for providing me with all of the performance management experiences to create this book. I bet most of you had no idea I was taking notes along the way.

About The Author

Tim Moran worked in Human Resources for 30+ years and for most of that time he felt like a fish out of water. He had very little patience for overly complicated HR processes and systems, believing they were detrimental to running an effective business and developing performance driven cultures. He was and is outspoken in his views.

In 2013, Tim started TMoran Consulting, LLC. As an independent HR Consultant he is focused on strategic human resource challenges facing client organizations. His approach is to understand the strategic direction of the business and then develop impactful people solutions to drive the success of the enterprise.

Prior to being an independent Consultant, Tim worked several years as a Human Resources Director for Hallmark Cards, Inc. Prior to Hallmark, he worked in human resource generalist and staffing related functions for NCR Corporation, Frito-Lay, Inc., Burke Energy Corp., and The Waterman Group.

He earned his bachelors degree in Psychology and his master's degree in Industrial and Organizational Psychology from Emporia State University, Emporia, Kansas.

Tim and his wife Pat live in Overland Park, Kansas. He has two children, Josh and Erika, and two dogs, Max and Tate. In addition to writing, speaking and HR consulting, his hobbies and interests include the University of Kansas basketball, gambling, and having a good time with family and friends.

You can connect with Tim via email or LinkedIn:

tmoranauthor728@yahoo.com

www.linkedin.com/pub/tim-moran/0/154/545/

References

(1) "The Blob." *Wikipedia The Free Encyclopedia.* 1 April 2013. 22 April 2013. http://en.wikipedia.org/wiki/The_Blob

(2) "Frederick Taylor and Scientific Management." *NetMBA Business Knowledge Center.* 24 April 2013 http://www.netmba.com/mgmt/scientific/

(3) "Frederick Taylor and Scientific Management." *NetMBA Business Knowledge Center.* 24 April 2013 http://www.netmba.com/mgmt/scientific/

(4) "Management by Objectives Law & Legal Definition." *US Legal.com.* 26 April 2013 http://definitions.uslegal.com/m/management-by-objectives/

(5) Morrison, Mike. "History of SMART Objectives." *RAPIDBI.com.* June 22, 2010. 28 April 2013 http://rapidbi.com/history-of-smart-objectives/

(6) "Big Data at the Speed of Business." *IBM.com.* 29 April 2013 http://www-01.ibm.com/software/data/bigdata/

(7) "Bear Stearns." *Wikipedia The Free Encyclopedia.* 30 April 2013 https://en.wikipedia.org/wiki/Bear_Stearns